Image Courtesy of the St James Missionary Society, Lima, Peru

Gerard Hanlon

Learning
from the
Poor

Reflections from a Shanty Town

Don Bosco Publications

Don Bosco Publications
Thornleigh House, Sharples Park, Bolton BL1 6PQ
United Kingdom

ISBN 978-1-909080-59-1
©Don Bosco Publications 2020
©Gerard Hanlon

The moral rights of the author have been asserted

All rights reserved. No part of this publication may be reproduced, stored in a retrieval system or transmitted in any form or by any means without the prior permission in writing of Don Bosco Publications. Enquiries concerning reproduction and requests for permissions should be sent to The Manager, Don Bosco Publications, at the address above.

Front cover photograph ©Giancarlo-Revolledo/unsplash

Printed in Malta by Melita Press

FSC
www.fsc.org
MIX
Paper from responsible sources
FSC® C110322

Acknowledgements

Some of the incidents mentioned in this book are used with permission from Novum Publishing and taken from the author's previous publication: Gerard Hanlon, *Peru Remembered*, London: Novum Publishing, 2019.

Bible references are taken from *The New Jerusalem Bible: Study Edition*, London: Darton, Longman & Todd Ltd., 1994.

While every effort has been made to trace references and acknowledge all copyright holders, we would like to apologise should there be any errors or omissions.

Contents

Introduction 1
Chapter One: The Poor 3
Chapter Two: The Poor of Our Time 11
Chapter Three: A New Way of Doing Theology 17
Chapter Four: Joy 21
Chapter Five: Hope and Patience 27
Chapter Six: Humility 31
Chapter Seven: Celebration 33
Chapter Eight: Family and Community 37
Chapter Nine: Communities of Faith 41
Chapter Ten: The Wisdom and Ingenuity of the Poor 45
Chapter Eleven: Environment 49
Chapter Twelve: Silence 53
Chapter Thirteen: Accompanying the Poor 57
Chapter Fourteen: Hospitality 59

Chapter Fifteen: Suffering 61
Chapter Sixteen: Death 65
Chapter Seventeen: Gracias 69
Chapter Eighteen: World Day of the Poor 71

Introduction

Pope Francis has said that the poor have much to teach us; what can we learn from them?

Since the second half of last century, poor peoples throughout the developing world have been abandoning their rural homes and fields and 'invading' the great cities. In Peru they lived in so called *'barriadas'*, now called 'human settlements', in Brazil, *'favelas'*. These enormous settlements are not slums, for a slum is a district which has deteriorated, and these 'slums of hope', as they have been called, are developing.

It has been my great good fortune to work as a missionary priest for over fifty years in Peru—in the *barriadas* of coastal Peru, with peasant farmers in remote Andean villages and in a city in the upper Amazon rainforest. Most of the people in these places were what we used to call 'the working classes'. Some were exceedingly poor.

In Peruvian shanty towns they were mostly peasants, or descendants of farmers, who had migrated to the city to start a new life—to find work, to build a home, to educate their children. In the Amazon many were riverside dwellers who had moved to the city.

The people among whom I worked were mostly Catholic people who welcomed the mainly foreign priests who moved in among them—patient with our struggle with a strange language and culture. They showed us great affection. They were a community who retained much of their ancient culture and customs but were now having to adapt to the urban struggle. They were men and women with young families, strangers to the city, socially marginalised there but who had many skills and great determination to begin a new life. They looked to the middle classes to employ them, and if they could not find work, they were infinitely resourceful in inventing jobs: selling trinkets on the streets, singing for a tip on buses, shoe-shining—whatever.

Many of the parishioners who attend my early Sunday Mass these days in the rather shabby urban sprawl of Lima are elderly and originally from highland provinces. They tend to be small in stature, wrinkled and infirm. A few have learning disabilities. They are not the totally abject poor, like the dying on the streets of Mother Teresa's Calcutta nor like a man whom a priest friend of mine picked up on the streets of Lima, cleaned him up and invited him to live in his house, because, as my friend told me, he would otherwise have died. But these people are struggling with life, and they remind us of the poor whom Jesus addressed in the Beatitudes.

The task of the Church and especially of missionaries is not so much to help the poor move into the middle classes but to guide them to understand that they are especially loved by God: "to bring good tidings to the poor".[1]

The poor are different from the rich and glamorous whose photographs fill glossy magazines and screens, but Pope Francis has said that the poor "have much to teach us",[2] and the great Archbishop Hélder Câmara of Brazil once commented: "I have learned much from those who are called poor but rich in the Holy Spirit". The poor evangelise us. Here are some of the things that one missionary has learned from them.

---

1   Cf. Isa 61:1; Lk 4:18.
2   Pope Francis: *Evangelii Gaudium—Joy of the Gospel*, (Vatican: Libreria Editrice Vaticana, 2013), n 198. (*EG*).

Chapter One

The Poor

Every tourist and pilgrim to the Holy Land returns home and tells of how they loved the region of Galilee. Perhaps they felt the spirit of Jesus sauntering along the lakeside or looking up at the great hills or gazing across the lake. It is a beautiful land and still sparsely inhabited. There is a hillside there which is called the Mount of the Beatitudes. Pilgrims and tourists visit it, and there is a church surrounded by gardens and quiet corners where Mass can be said, as I have done on a couple of occasions. The ground falls away, across stony fields, to the lake below, and one thinks there of the Beatitudes and the lilies of the field.

Blessed are the poor in spirit, for theirs is the kingdom of heaven.[1]

Blessed are you poor, for yours is the kingdom of God.[2]

In the Old Testament the "poor" meant the pious,[3] and one Greek lexicon translates the New Testament word πτωχόι as 'beggars', those who live the lives of poor men but, referring to our texts, this lexicon adds "not those who are merely poor in material things, but humble, devout persons, who feel the need of God's help." So the *ptochoi*, which in Aramaic, the language of Jesus, were

---

1 Matt 5:3.
2 Lk 6:20.
3 Isa 61:1.

the humble people who understood that they were nothing themselves: the childlike.[4] They were not the *learned and the clever* but those without hope in society yet open to hope in something greater. The majority of people in the Galilee of Jesus' time were labourers, who worked the land for landowners, and fishermen, shepherds or craftsmen. Though Jesus himself and his disciples were perhaps themselves not reduced to begging, they belonged to these working and humbler classes. Below these were the beggars, the lepers, the outcasts. Jesus felt that he was especially called and "anointed to preach the good news"[5] to all these humbler classes.[6]

Perhaps the individual Beatitudes were pronounced by Jesus at different times then collected and assembled together by the Gospel writers, but what interests us here is what Jesus meant by the poor and why he said they are happy (μακάριοι).

Matthew's Gospel imagines Jesus as the new Moses announcing a new code from a hillside. Luke has the scene on a plain.[7] And Matthew's Gospel adds "in spirit" to the first Beatitude perhaps in an attempt to interpret the harshness of Luke's Beatitude.[8] Scripture scholars believe that Luke's starker version represented Jesus' original words.

Can we recognise in Matthew's "in spirit" a correct interpretation? Though perhaps not exactly what Jesus said, "in spirit" has the meaning of "willingly". Such people do not rejoice in their worldly goods, they look for something beyond; they are more likely to rejoice in the good news of the Gospel. The Beatitude is saying that if you are poor, you are fortunate because it is easier for you to understand what the Kingdom of God is all about. The poor are those who, more easily than others, realise that they cannot do without God. Someone has said that those who have got rid of false illusions, obligations, commitments and burdens are the truly poor because they are free. And

---

4   Matt 11:25.
5   Cf. Lk 4:18.
6   In the ancient world, Christianity was the only movement that was concerned with poor people, which was the majority at that time. They were the fragile, dependent ones in society and with little influence.
7   Lk 6:17.
8   Pope Francis comments that in speaking simply of poverty Luke invites us to a life of austerity and renouncement, c.f. Pope Francis, *Gaudete et Exsultate— Rejoice and be Glad*, (Vatican: Libreria Editrice Vaticana, 2018),n. 70. (*GE*).

William Barclay[9] reminds us that Jesus is not praising a situation of living in the slums or suffering hunger but of a poverty of those who rely on God.[10] The Beatitudes tell us that the poor are to be especially congratulated, not because they are morally better than others but because it is easier for them to listen attentively to the good news and accept it—unlike many of the influential people of Jerusalem and the rich and powerful of today. The 'little people' are getting the message because they are aware of their need. Jesus announces that there is a new possibility of salvation for them. His words are words of encouragement. Though poverty in itself is not a 'good', much less so destitution, Jesus showed how poverty, lowliness and childlikeness are necessary to embrace the Kingdom and its values. He had a special affection for society's poor and marginalised. He was on their side, and had, what is called in our time 'a preferential option for the poor'. All his teaching and healings show empathy for the poor and afflicted (e.g. the widow's mite, the paralysed man, the mother of the dead young man of Naim, etc.). His alleviation of the poor's burdens and his healing of the sick are signs that the Kingdom is coming for them: "The good news is proclaimed to the poor"[11] so "Go back and tell John what you have seen and heard: the blind see, the lame walk."[12] Thus the first Beatitude is a word of congratulation: how fortunate are you the lowly, little people of the servile classes.

Fr Gustavo Gutiérrez[13] calls them the "insignificant people"; for Jesus, they are the privileged heirs of the Kingdom. So, the poor can be happy and blessed (*makarioi*). Their only reliance is on God, for they have no other. Though they struggle for the necessities of life, they are not distracted by riches.[14] In his

---

9   W. Barclay, *The Gospel according to Matthew*, (Westminster: John Knox Press, 2001).
10   "There is no justification," writes Dietrich Bonhoeffer, "for setting Luke's version of the Beatitudes over against Matthew's. Matthew is not spiritualising the Beatitudes, and Luke giving them in their original form. Both gospels recognise that neither privation nor renunciation…is justified, except by the call and promise of Jesus…who is the sole ground of their Beatitude." D. Bonhoeffer, *The Cost of Discipleship*, (London: SCM Press, 1959), 96.
11   Lk 4:18.
12   Lk 11:5.
13   Gustavo Gutiérrez Merino OP (born 8 June 1928) is a Peruvian philosopher, theologian, and Dominican priest regarded as one of the founders of liberation theology.
14   'The poor' was a term used of the pious in the Old Testament and seems to have become a self-designation of certain Jews in the period after the Old Testament.

book 'God of Surprises',[15] Gerard Hughes described the poor as "those who know their own emptiness and throw themselves on the mercy of God". They have an advantage over the rich: it is easier for the poor to accept the challenge of the Kingdom. Francis of Assisi understood this and embraced radical poverty. Men and women who enter religious orders do not live in destitution, but they opt to "seek first the kingdom of God".[16] Such people are fortunate because they are in a position to understand what is truly important. It is the paradox of poverty.

The relation between God and the poor impregnates the Bible.[17] A glance at the whole Bible will convince us that God has a special interest in and love for them.[18] The Exodus narrative is the story of Yahweh's intervention to relieve the Hebrews of political slavery. Jesus, in the tradition of Israel's ancient prophets, inherits their attitudes and themes and, in spite of all other concerns in the apostolic church, the first Christians were "to remember to help the poor."[19]

Christian theology teaches that God's love is infinite and for all people, but the life of Jesus shows a special affection for those who don't count in society, for the little people. When he visited the synagogue at Nazareth, he quoted Isaiah:[20] "The Spirit of the Lord God is upon me because the Lord has anointed me to bring good tidings to the poor."[21] The poor have the good news preached to them,[22] and they will "inherit the earth."[23] Jesus seemed pleased that he was surrounded by the poor. The term 'poor' originally meant those who had no inheritance of their own, those who were in economic need and also those who had a low and insignificant social status.[24]

Cf. J.C. Fenton: *Saint Matthew (Pelican Gospel Commentaries)*, (London: Penguin Books, 1963), 80.

15   G.W. Hughes, *God of Surprises*, (London: Darton Longman & Todd, 2008).
16   Matt 6:33.
17   Examples: Isa 61:1–2; Eccl 11:12, et al.
18   Cf. Isa 61:1–2 and Eccl 11:12 talk about those who are "rich in poverty."
19   Gal 2:10.
20   Isa 61:1.
21   Lk 4:18.
22   Matt 11:5.
23   Cf. Ps 37:11.
24   J.J. Kanagaraj, 'The Poor in the Gospels and the Good News Proclaimed to Them' in *Themelios*, 23(1). Online: https://themelios.thegospelcoalition.org/article/the-poor-in-the-gospels-and-the-good-news-proclaimed-to-them/ [Accessed 16/03/2020].

Jesus turned the established religion of his time on its head. It has been said that he 'declared war' on the materialism of his day seeing mammon[25] as a rival god. Instead of preaching fasting, prayer, ritual purity and observance of the Law, he profaned the Sabbath, ate with sinners and publicans, forgave in God's name, touched the ritually impure, said that prostitutes would enter the Kingdom and criticised religious officials![26] Jesus announced an upside down kingdom! Christianity turns everything on its head. The values and conditions of a prosperous and comfortable life are reversed. On judgment day, those who are now at the bottom of the pile may well be at the top. The poor and meek, who are at the bottom of society, will be at the summit in God's Kingdom.

Although it seems that the poor have the advantage over the rich and powerful, symbolising the kind of people who will enter the Kingdom, what then does Jesus offer to those who are not so poor, those who are comfortably off, socially recognised and influential? What are they to do?[27] And what would he say to the super rich who have wealth beyond all wildest dreams or those who hoard luxury goods?

Though Jesus is the Messiah of the poor, he didn't spurn the better off if they were good people: he sat at table with the fairly well-to-do (Zachaeus for example) and did not condemn them. For although Jesus did invite the rich young man to renounce his wealth, he doesn't seem to have so challenged everyone. He was all things to all people, yet he had a severe warning to the avaricious and those who trust in their riches: "How hard it is for those who have riches to enter the kingdom of God."[28] The rich young man's problem was his dependence on his riches; he was secure with them and self-sufficient.

---

25   A Chaldee or Syriac word meaning "wealth" or "riches" (Lk 16:9-11).
26   Something similar happened in the Latin American Church last century when the rich and respectable, as well as Church authorities, couldn't cope with the new theology of the poor. It is also happening today under the papacy of Pope Francis.
27   Ancient Israel saw poverty as a misfortune and riches a result of fidelity to God, as do Calvinists today. Prov 6:6-11 condemns idleness. The Bible also sometimes sees poverty as the result of injustice: Amos 2:6f; 4:1; 5:11; Eze 22:29, or as the abuse of power: Amos 5:7, Jer 34:8-22. The Fathers of the Church struggled with the notion of evangelical poverty. They tried to strike a balance between wealth, which they could not simply condemn, and poverty which they found difficult to idealise. Occasionally they romanticised poverty while admitting it was a bitter trial.
28   Mk 10:23.

"Woe to you who are rich"[29] who refuse to commit yourselves to Kingdom values, who are content with your wealth and comfort. Such are those who are condemned in the Gospel.

For Our Life

The God of the Bible, who rescued the people of Israel from slavery in Egypt, and who in Jesus had showed a 'preferential option for the poor', invites men and women today, through the example of Pope Francis, to ask how it is that a minority of people enjoy unbelievable riches while three billion live on less than $2.50 a day and some 1.3 billion—74% of humankind—on less than $1.25.

All are challenged: "Seek ye first the kingdom of God."[30] The self-sufficient are not open to God's future. For the person who is poor in the Gospel sense, the things of God's Kingdom are their riches.

God never fails the poor: Isaiah 58:6–7, I Corinthians 5:11, Ephesians 5:5, I Timothy 6:17–19. In our 'must-have generation' we are bombarded by advertising for the new things, for the latest mobile phone, domestic appliance or gadget. Pope Francis calls us to try to live more simply. If we do first seek the Kingdom of God with all our heart, material things will fall into place. In his Apostolic Exhortation *Gaudete et Exsultate* Pope Francis says that:

> This spiritual poverty is closely linked to what St Ignatius of Loyola calls "Holy indifference", which brings us to a radiant interior freedom: "We need to train ourselves to be indifferent in our attitude to all created things, in all that is permitted to our free will and not forbidden; so that on our part, we do not set our hearts on good health rather than bad, riches rather than poverty, honour rather than dishonour, a long life rather than a short one, and so in all the rest."[31]
>
> Luke does not speak of poverty "of spirit" but simply of those who are "poor" (cf. Lk 6:20). In this way, he too invites us to live a plain and austere life.[32]

---

29   Lk 6:24.
30   Matt 6:33.
31   *GE*, n 69.
32   ibid., n 70.

The self-sufficient are not open to God's future. For the person who is poor in the Gospel sense, the things of God's Kingdom are their riches.

However, making a radical option for the poor can provoke the enmity of the wealthy and powerful, as happened in Latin America.

To serve the poor wholeheartedly, we would have to become poor ourselves! For middle-class Christians from prosperous societies, this is not easy. We cannot serve the poor from on high, so we might have to simplify our lives, do away with what is not necessary, eat more frugally, share what we have, limit the cult of shopping for 'nice things', accept the poverty of sickness, disabilities and ageing, the loss of friends, the inability to work or function normally, to be unable to travel or to move around.

Chapter Two

The Poor of Our Time

One cannot travel far in Latin America before spotting the huge shanty towns ('human settlements' or 'young towns' in Peru, *favelas* in Brazil) that ring the great cities. And their story is just as interesting and important as the Inca ruins of Machu Picchu!

The people of the shanty towns are not simply those who lack money and whose opinion does not count. They are those who do not speak good Spanish or do not have white skins. They are the marginalised. They are the poor women from mountain provinces or farmers with gnarled hands, ponchos and rolled-up trousers who can still be seen in mountain towns, those who have to struggle for their rights as they demand reasonable wages, housing and amenities. For those who will listen they are the voice of God, clamouring to evangelise the rich and powerful.

The one-time Anglican bishop of Liverpool, David Shepherd, once said that poverty is not only about the shortage of money; it is about relationships, about how people are treated, about powerlessness, exclusion and the lack of dignity.[1] And Pope Francis, in his introduction to a book written by Fr Gustavo

---

1   Archbishop of Canterbury's Advisory Group on Urban Priority Areas (ACUPA), *Faith in the City: A Call for Action by Church and Nation*, (London: Church House Publishing, 1985).

Gutiérrez and Cardinal Müller wrote: "The Western world sees poverty primarily as the absence of economic power"[2] but the theological notion of poverty is not just about those who lack money; it is also about those who have no voice, whose opinion is insignificant in society, who have no say in public affairs; they are the 'unheard'.[3]

The poor are those who are the first to suffer in earthquakes, flash floods and ecological despoliation, because their badly built homes are fragile, often built on precarious hills or on land sought after by mining and logging companies. Today they are the socially marginalised, the refugees, the ragpickers, the homeless (and also those who sleep under London's arches) and the shanty town dwellers of developing countries. Two thousand years after Jesus' words, the poor are still with us, millions more than in his time: "you always have the poor with you."[4]

Not everyone was happy about the new, so-called 'liberation theology'[5] which began to be taught some decades ago: there was strong opposition to it among the better off, the powerful and the more traditionally minded theologians. Mahatma Gandhi once said: "Those who say religion has nothing to do with politics do not know what religion means".[6] The new theology in Latin America provided a voice for the voiceless, especially the urban poor, and they clamoured to be heard. A notable example was that of an invasion on the desert hills on the south side of Lima in the early 1970s, which involved the death of a young person, the police detention of a supportive bishop and the intervention of the cardinal archbishop. It resulted in the government assigning land to the homeless and the armed forces helping the homeless to move on to the vacant land! It was liberation theology in practice; the hierarchical Church was now on the side of the poor. In later times Pope John Paul II and Cardinal Ratzinger both visited Villa el Salvador on the outskirts of Lima. I heard that the cardinal was deeply moved by the poverty he saw.

---

2   G. H. Müller and G. Gutiérrez, *Iglesia pobre y para los pobres*, (Madrid: San Pablo Comunicacion SSP, 2014), 9.
3   ibid.
4   Matt 26:11; Mk 14:7; Jn 12:8.
5   A movement in Christian theology, developed mainly by Latin American Roman Catholics, which attempts to address the problems of poverty and social injustice as well as spiritual matters.
6   Online: https://www.mkgandhi.org/momgandhi/chap18.htm [Accessed 02/04/2020].

Still today, despite much progress, 30% of Peruvians are classed as living in poverty and some 13% still live in extreme poverty mainly in the cold sierras. And there are the millions of people who once lived in remote villages in the highlands but who have moved to the great coastal cities or emerged from the jungles to live in the towns of Peru in search of better things. All these people usually began their new life in straw huts but over the years have built more solid homes, perhaps have found work and brought up a new generation, yet they still lead frugal lives on the margins of the more prosperous classes.

They are not angels: many abuse alcohol whenever there is a pretext for a 'fiesta'; there is a high incidence of marital infidelity and an exaggerated affection for mothers yet abuse and disrespect for other women. They have had to learn to survive in a society which favours the rich and powerful, so they have learned to manipulate the system, to bend the rules wherever possible: a back-hander to a policeman to avoid a motoring fine, a request to a relative or friend in high places to obtain a favour, a battle to steal land to build their homes.

In spite of Thomas Merton's comment that "we experience God in proportion as we are stripped and emptied of attachment to his creatures",[7] people need the basics of life and security. Capitalism has created a world of overwhelming contrasts: the almost beyond-belief riches of the few whose super yachts and luxury homes contrast with the millions who live in shanty towns, on refuse dumps and in immigrant camps.

But who would want to be poor, abandoned, marginalised, a nobody? Only the great saints have understood the Christian challenge: that we are nothing, that we cannot exist without God and that all we have and are is from Him.

Simone Weil wrote that "we only possess what we renounce".[8] The poor haven't renounced anything and they long for things. Yet in one sense they own all things because they are loved by God: "having nothing but own everything."[9]

---

[7] T. Merton, *New Seeds of Contemplation*, (New York: New Directions, 2007), 268.

[8] S. Weil, *Gravity and Grace*, translated by E. Crawford, (London: Routledge and Kegan Paul Ltd, 1952), 30.

[9] II Cor 6:10.

However, poor people want to rise from their poverty! Many would like to emulate the rich and enjoy their benefits. When I travel abroad, my less fortunate friends in Peru say to me "put me in your suitcase"; they would love to live in Miami!

Many Peruvian families whose parents 'invaded' the empty desert land fifty years ago and at first lived in a shack on the desert floor may by now, if they and their children have work, be dwelling in a brick and cement house with decent furniture, modern appliances and perhaps a car. The ground floor will be inhabited by the parents, the second floor by their married children and so on up the storeys. They are no longer extremely poor, though they may retain the spirit of the poor for they have known poverty.

Those who join a religious congregation take a vow of poverty. They renounce private property. But their lives are usually quite comfortable, and all is provided: food, shelter and health care. There are few who have the courage to emulate Francis of Assisi or Charles de Foucauld.

So, who are the poor today? Who are those who seek first the Kingdom of God, who put this before all else? They are the ones who live in the world needing life's basic necessities, but their true values are Kingdom values. They realise that they need God more than anything else and they can accommodate their lives to prosperity or necessity, to health or suffering, to life or death.

The reign (or Kingdom of God) is not a place of course, nor a specific time, but a situation in the future but which has already begun. "The kingdom of God is at hand."[10] It is a state of affairs, an attitude, a way of life, a society (and hopefully a Church) in which God rules; a new future in which men and women lead a new life under the sovereignty of God. The Beatitudes are a pre-condition for entry into God's reign. What is demanded is to give our heart to God not to possessions, influence or power. "Do not lay up for yourselves treasures on earth."[11] It is a matter of a state of mind. No worldly enslavement but to be ready, waiting and watching for the Kingdom. The poor and meek are fortunate now not merely in the future. So, we must study them and learn from them.

---

10 Mk 1:15.
11 Matt 6:19.

Resolution

How can we live a life of simplicity in a world of consumerism, ever more appliances and the temptation of advertising?

Do my religious devotions prevent me from a serious commitment to the poor?

Could I do something to alleviate the poor in my neighbourhood?

"Whenever our interior life becomes caught up in its own interests and concerns, there is no room for others, no place for the poor" writes Pope Francis.[12] The truth is hidden from those who are absorbed in their personal concerns, their personal progress, social status or careers and from those who pretend to be 'wise', who think they know everything.

---

12   *EG*, n 2.

Chapter Three

A New Way of Doing Theology

High in the mountains of Peru one still meets the peasant farmers who live in small huts along with their animals, walk the great hills in bare feet and are far from amenities, especially hospitals. In Peru they are the 'native peoples', descendants of the Inca empire. And the Latin America church has now opted for them.

The Latin American theologian Segundo Galilea said that previously "the Gospel in Latin America failed to create justice for the oppressed."[1] But happily, in the middle of the last century, the Church in that subcontinent began to concern itself with the poor.

Liberation theology was not thought up by the poor but by Church personnel who worked among them. It arose because a few insightful bishops and theologians saw the oppression and neglect of the majority of the people by great landowners, international companies, politicians and oligarchies in Latin America. What struck these Church workers was the 'adjacency' of rich and poor in Latin America: great wealth alongside extreme poverty. It was the poor who maintained the wealthy in their social niche and who often lived near them, around the great haciendas in the Peruvian highlands or, as time went

---

1   S. Galilea, *The Beatitudes: To Evangelize as Jesus Did*, translated by R.R. Barr, (Maryknoll, New York: Orbis books, 1984).

on, who lived in despicable slums in the inner cities or in the growing shanty towns which ringed the great cities. Thus, it was, as so often, the structures of society which caused great poverty; it has been called 'social sin', causing poverty, oppression, hunger, unemployment, sickness and premature death.

The Church in Latin America had tried to evangelise the rural peoples by sending missionaries into remote areas: in the sixteenth century the great Archbishop of Lima, Toribio de Mogrovejo, had sent his priests into the mountains armed with a simple catechism for the barely literate, and there had been a kind of native 'upland clergy' who had attended the traditional Iberian-type feasts of remote villages, administering the sacraments and doing what they could to evangelise the locals. There had even been rural catechists, often blind men, who learned and taught the faith by rote. But the poor were only recipients of doctrine. If they organised their own patronal feasts, it was often mixed with folklore and jovial festivity. They were not involved in theological or social reflection. "The custom is the law," the people used to say to us in the highlands of Peru. Meanwhile, Church hierarchy and the monastic order in the cities were comfortable with the urban middle classes, the wealthy and the powerful.

Traditional scholastic theology had been divided up into treatises: *De Deo Uno*, *De Incarnatione*, etc. Truth would be expounded, and conclusions drawn. The new theology of the Third World turned this upside down: it began with a reflection on social reality and then moved on to conclusions. It marked a shift from a deductive theology—from revealed truths—to an inductive one which began not with the great Christian truths but with the social situation.[2] The Church must become "incarnate in their [the poor] world, proclaiming good news to them, giving them hope, …defending their cause and share their fate" wrote St Óscar Romero.[3] The poor themselves were invited to create 'church' for which they were responsible. It was not merely an attempt to change society but also to live out their faith in a new way—in sharing, in prayer, in cooperative development. They become 'evangelisers'.

---

2   While Western theology was concerned about explaining the truths of faith, liberation theology is interested in real life. One doesn't learn about liberation theology; one does it. The doing is the learning.

3   Ó. Romero, *Voice of the Voiceless: The Four Pastoral Letters and Other Statements*, translated by M.J. Walsh, (Maryknoll, New York: Orbis Books, 1985), 182.

The bishops of Latin America, at their meeting in Medellín, Colombia in 1968 spoke of the 'institutionalised violence' of the State, Latin American oligarchies, the military, the more powerful countries of the North and even the traditional Church which had worked happily alongside these elements.[4] Bishops, theologians and many religious personnel took a new stand alongside the poor and marginalised peoples of the subcontinent. The Church, especially those members of it who worked among the poor, became critical of a 'European theology' which had been too theoretical and removed from real life. The great issues in Latin America and indeed in other developing countries were poverty, underdevelopment, exploitation, injustice and dependency. They were concerned to liberate the poor and marginalised peoples from physical, spiritual and social marginalisation and oppression. It was new way of 'doing theology' and it was not confined solely to theologians: the people themselves were involved in it as 'theologians'. The Bible was read from the point of view of the poor and oppressed, and it looked rather different from previous readings. The Exodus story was seen as a political liberation on the part of Yahweh for his oppressed people. And so was born a new and beautiful relationship with the poor and especially with the poor of the shanty settlements. "The contemplation of Christ in the suffering and oppressed…is the historical content of Christian contemplation in the Latin American church" wrote the liberation theologian Segundo Galilea.[5] St Óscar Romero went so far as to claim that it is impossible to call oneself a Christian unless one assumes a preferential option for the poor. And so, in this huge subcontinent we think a great deal about poverty and the poor.

Then, the Latin American bishops, at their next meeting in Puebla, Mexico in 1979, opted for the "young people and children, native peoples, peasants and workers, the under-employed, the marginalised and the elderly".[6] The new theology was the voice of those without a voice. These classes were in the majority as were the masses in the time of Jesus. The poor were being 'concientised', shown why they were poor and why they were victims of

---

4   Cf. General Conclusion of the Medellin International Study Week 1968, in M. Warren (ed.), *Sourcebook for Modern Catechetics*, (Winona, Minnesota: St Mary's Press: Christian Brothers Publications, 1997).
5   S. Galilea, *Following Jesus,* translated by Sr Helen Phillips, MM, (Maryknoll, New York: Orbis Books, 1981).
6   The Latin American Episcopal Council (CELAM) III, *Conferencia General del Episcopado Latinoamericano (Puebla)*, (Bogotà: CELAM, 1979), 31-39.

an unjust social system where the wealth was in the hands of the few rich and powerful.

Wealthy citizens and members of the powerful social classes became alarmed at the talk of liberation theology for it apparently had links with Marxism (arising from a 'social analysis'). It also seemed to threaten their status. They saw a Church that was opting for the poor and asked, "What about us?"

When I first went to Peru, some ninety families ran the great haciendas and enterprises. The ninety families represented much less than 1% of the Peruvian population. As in ancient Israel,[7] so many of the rich lived in luxury without concern for the poor, the old and the sick.

Liberation theology has reminded us that service to the poor is at the centre of our faith. The great saints knew this and were of service to them, but the new theology put the whole Christian community on the side of the poor, not just to help them, but to accompany them and to live and learn from them. St Paul told his readers never to be condescending to the poor but to make real friends of them,[8] and that is what so many missionaries to South America were happy to do.

Resolution

Can we learn from the poor?

How should Christians today announce the good news to the poor?

---

7 Isa 3:16f; 5:1f, 20–23.
8 Rom 12:16.

Chapter Four

Joy

Brethren be joyful[1]
Charity, joy, peace, patience[2]
Come ring out our joy to the Lord[3]
I have told you this so that my own joy may be in you[4]

I once showed an English bishop around a parish in a young town (a onetime shanty), where I had worked many years previously. The parish sisters had formed women's groups which produced beautiful garments and artefacts for export, thereby earning the ladies a small remuneration. Small in stature, the women beamed up at the tall bishop, and one of them said: "We have nothing to give you, but we can share with you our joy."

The poor are usually delighted to see the stranger or a foreigner. They give you a warm smile—though their smiles often hide poverty and suffering. I always found them ready to smile and enjoy a little joke. In spite of their huge personal problems, they maintain their good humour in public. At the end of Sunday Mass or parish meeting, there is always a smile and warm handshake.

---

1 II Cor 13:11.
2 Gal 5.15.
3 Ps 94:1.
4 Jn 15:11.

The poor tend to be very courteous. In Latin America one always shakes hands on meeting and parting from a person. In some parts it is customary to make a cheek to cheek greeting, and parents insist that their small children so greet even a complete stranger. Rudeness, except when a man is drunk, is extremely rare among the poor. The peasant women of the Andes have great charm. Small things amuse them and shopping in their Indian markets can be a delightful experience.

I suspect that, despite great suffering and overwhelming problems, there is much joy among the shanty town peoples of the world. Life can be dull in the gloomy, damp weather (at least in the long winter months of coastal Peru) together with the routine of work in the big city—in factories, on the streets and buses. Many have to travel such long distances that they make up for lack of sleep by sleeping on their journeys. Is it any wonder that these people welcome any excuse for a fiesta or a laugh? They do not understand moroseness: "Why are you sad?" they ask if you are not smiling!

It is astonishing how often the idea of joy occurs in the Bible. I think it was Pope John Paul II who pointed this out. There is no doubt that Christianity is meant to be a religion of joy. Pope Francis' very first letter to the world was all about joy:

> The Gospel...constantly invites us to rejoice. ..."Rejoice!" is the angel's greeting to Mary (Lk 1:28). Mary's visit to Elizabeth makes John leap for joy in his mother's womb (cf. Lk 1:41). In her song of praise, Mary proclaims: "My spirit rejoices in God my Saviour" (Lk 1:47). When Jesus begins his ministry, John cries out: "For this reason, my joy has been fulfilled" (Jn 3:29). Jesus himself "rejoiced in the Holy Spirit" (Lk 10:21). His message brings us joy: "I have said these things to you, so that my joy may be in you, and that your joy may be complete" (Jn 15:11). Our Christian joy drinks of the wellspring of his brimming heart. He promises his disciples: "You will be sorrowful, but your sorrow will turn into joy" (Jn 16:20).[5]

Francis opens this exhortation by saying that, "The joy of the gospel fills the hearts and lives of those who accept [the] offer of salvation [and] are set free from sin, sorrow, inner emptiness and loneliness".[6] It has been said that this document initiated a new tone in the papacy. Francis accuses some

---

5   *EG*, n 5.
6   ibid., n 1.

Christians of living in Lent rather than Easter and reproaches modern society of providing pleasure but not joy.[7] A little later in the document the Pope says: "The most beautiful and natural expressions of joy I have seen in my life were in poor people who had little to hang on to".[8] But then Francis had worked in Latin America!

Christian joy does not mean hilarity but a deep-rooted contentment, a calm outlook amid the rough and tumble of life. It means joy because God loves us. Perhaps this is what Julian of Norwich meant when she wrote that "All will be well, all manner of things will be well"—a phrase that has become popular in our time.[9] It is a peaceful conviction and tranquillity because we believe that God is on our side, that he loves us as no one else can love us and is ready to forgive everything.

Did Jesus ever smile? It has been said that the Jews of Jesus' time had little humour. Perhaps they rarely laughed outright. But Jesus must have smiled when he embraced the children, for children communicate joy. And when Jesus spoke of the Kingdom and heaven, he used the image of a meal: "The kingdom of heaven may be compared to a king who gave a feast".[10] He even enjoyed meals with the better off.[11] In spite of what Paul says about it not being "in eating and drinking that makes the kingdom of God but…in joy",[12] when you are invited to a meal you don't go with a gloomy face, you chat and smile. Have you ever noticed the faces of people as they enter a restaurant? You don't go as an invited guest to a meal with a long face!

So, what does the Bible mean by 'joy'? Christian joy has nothing to do with fun. When we meet a very good person, we can sense a tranquillity and joy in their countenance. Underlying it may be great suffering but that does not surface.

---

7 ibid., n 7.
8 ibid.
9 Julian, Anchoress at Norwich, *Revelations of Divine Love recorded 1373*, translated by G. Warrack for the British Museum, (London: Methuen & Company, 1901), 56.
10 Matt 22:2.
11 Lk 14:19.
12 Rom 14:17.

Perhaps we think of St Paul as rather a serious fellow: a trained Pharisee and intellectual, but his letters frequently speak of joy: "Be joyful in hope" he tells the Romans[13] and he wrote to the Galatians telling them to "shout for joy".[14] His letter to the Philippians makes frequent mention of joy: he himself is full of joy and prays for his readers with joy;[15] he tells them to be full of joy[16] and says that they will have the joy of welcoming Epaphroditus who is being sent to them.[17] So perhaps Paul wasn't a 'joker', but he understood the deep joy of the Gospel message.[18] The Acts of the Apostles speak of the joy of the first Christians.[19]

I once knew a great Christian man who died with the words: "Cry out with joy to the Lord" on his lips.

St Francis of Assisi is the saint of joy and was a bit of a joker. He was once out walking with one of his brothers and as they approached a monastery to seek a bed for the night, he said to his companion: "Wouldn't it be wonderful if they shut the door in our faces!" A bit mad but a happy man! And perhaps that is what is meant by Christian joy: happiness. Simone Weil believed that joy was a gateway to God.[20]

Related to joy is cheerfulness. I found the poor very cheerful. They are delighted to meet you, especially if you are a foreigner, they have great interest in you. Their greetings show this: *Buenos días, tanto gusto de conocerlo*— Good day, so pleased to meet you. Latin America is a 'personalistic' society: people are more important than things. Anglo-Saxon peoples ask: "What do you do?" Latin Americans ask: "Who are you, where do you come from?" We might ask which is the most Christian question.

It is a great joy to be with and to serve the poor, to give and receive, to laugh and to cry with them; to accept their simple hospitality, to sit in their homes,

---

13   Rom 12:12.
14   Gal 4:27.
15   Phil 4:10; 1:4.
16   Phil 4:4.
17   Phil 2:29.
18   Cf. Rom 14:17; II Cor 6:10; Phil 1:4.
19   Acts 2:46.
20   Cf. S. Weil, *Gateway to God*, translated by D. Raper, (London: HarperCollins, 1974).

to eat their food, to put up with lesser hygiene than we would like, to shake their gnarled and perhaps dirty hands, to risk infection and to welcome them into our own homes.

But we must show respect to the poor. The poor are often deferential, they lack the confidence and self-sufficiency of the better off, one of whose temptations is arrogance. It is sad to hear, as sometimes happens, a more affluent person or foreigner shout at poor workmen. We must never be condescending either but make real friends of them: "Pay no regard to social standing but meet humble people on their own terms" wrote Paul to the Romans.[21] We must make real friends of them.

Desmond Tutu and the Dalai Lama wrote 'The Book of Joy'[22] which tells of their week together in search of joy. The bishop said that joy did not mean happiness but something much bigger in spite of life's tragedies and sorrows. "As we discover more joy, we can face suffering in a way that enables rather than embitters; we have heartbreak with being broken."[23] And the Dalai Lama said that "from the moment of birth every human being wants to discover happiness…from the very core of our being we simply desire joy."[24]

Pope Francis has said that "a Christian is never bored or sad. Rather, the one who loves Christ is full of joy and radiates joy",[25] and the saint is able to live with joy and a sense of humour.[26] If we are not joyful, we are not following Christ fully. Those who have totally handed over their lives to God are happy.

Resolution

If the Gospel is good news, then it should produce joy.

---

21 Rom 12:16.
22 Dalai Lama, D. Tutu and D. Abrams (ed.), The Book of Joy: Lasting Happiness in a Changing World, (London: Penguin Random House, 2016).
23 ibid., 12.
24 ibid., 14.
25 Pope Francis (@Pontifex), June 30, 2013 "A Christian is never bored or sad. Rather, the one who loves Christ is full of joy and radiates joy." [Tweet] https://twitter.com/pontifex/status/351286563709263876?lang=en
26 *GE*, n 122.

Pope Francis has said that "the identity card of a Christian is their joy, the joy of the Gospel."[27] He does not, of course, eliminate the cross.

Try to live a life of inner joy and radiate it to others.

---

27   Pope Francis, *Ode to Joy: Morning Meditation in the Chapel of the Domus Sanctae Marthae*, Monday May 23, 2016, (Vatican: Libreria Editrice Vaticana).

Chapter Five

Hope and Patience

The joys and hopes, the grievances and the anxieties of the men of this age, especially those who are poor or in any way afflicted, these too are the joys and hopes, the griefs and anxieties of the followers of Christ.[1]

Charity, joy, peace, patience[2]

Mañana (tomorrow) is one of the most frequently spoken words among the Peruvian poor. It not only means 'tomorrow' but 'sometime in the future'. In offices, hospitals, schools, to be told that your request or appointment will be attended to *mañana*, means you will have to return, hopefully, perhaps a few more times.

My parishioners often said to me: "One must have faith", I think they not only meant hope, but also patience. If you live at the top of desert hill without electricity, piped water or sewage and a long walk down the hill to the bus stop, then you must have patience, waiting one day for better things. The poor of the urban settlements can teach us about patience.

---

1   Paul VI, *Gaudium et Spes—Joy and Hope*, (Vatican: Libreria Editrice Vaticana), n 1. (*GS*).
2   Gal 5:22–23.

Of the three cardinal virtues, faith, hope and charity, hope, sandwiched between faith and love is less talked about than the others. Perhaps it is too much like faith. It is difficult, sometimes to distinguish it from faith. In fact, Pope Benedict XVI, in his encyclical *Spes salvi*,[3] pointed out that in many instances, 'hope' does mean 'faith'. Hope is to do with expectancy and "the distinguishing mark of Christians is that they have a future."[4] Hope means the assurance of things promised. It sustains our faith. St Paul reminded the Ephesians that prior to their conversion they were without hope, but not now as Christians[5], as "we are saved by hope".[6] It is the gateway to eternal bliss.

The poor are full of hope—for better things. It has to be their outlook on life. The poor of the shanty towns are there because of their hope for a new life in the city—better education for their children, jobs, a new house, a car, access to hospitals and an upward move to the middle classes. You cannot live in a small hut lacking amenities without anticipating better things. The material hope of the poor is a symbol of a deeper Christian sentiment or virtue: "we hope for grace and for glory" as an old prayer had it.

My parishioners had to learn to wait. Waiting, standing in long queues, building for the future, are part of the life of the poor.

There were no short cuts for them for they had little influence and no friends in high places. The first shanty town dwellers in Lima came from mountain provinces where life was slow. From this, they had learned patience, which enabled them to cope with their slow integration into the city, as those who 'invade' land don't have immediate access to water, light or sanitation. It takes at least twenty years or more for a family that began a new life in a Peruvian shanty town for them to build up to a brick/cement house with furniture and some modern appliances.

Yet the temptation for the poor is to emulate the more comfortably off and to enter a culture of materialism. I once went into a straw hut where the only piece of furniture was a huge, new television. I commented on it and the lady

---

3   Benedict XVI, *Spes salvi—Saved in Hope*, (Vatican: Libreria Editrice Vaticana, 2007). (SS).
4   ibid., n 2.
5   Eph 2:12; cf. I Thess 4:13.
6   Rom 8:24.

replied: "Yes, Padre, just to have something." But in general, though the poor yearn for the good things of life, they make do with what they have.

In their previous, rural areas, life was cyclical: the annual routine of crops and fiestas. In the city their life is lineal: it has to move forward to better things as they struggle to progress. Yet in spite of their poverty, I don't think the poor despair or complain. Their outlook is positive. Their aim is to become more affluent, of course, but they don't seem obsessed with consumerism; their concerns are work, the daily bread, the family and health.

Many of those in poverty do progress materially, though it takes perhaps two or three generations. I now am asked to bless the new cars of people whose parents or grandparents emigrated from remote rural villages to the shanty towns of the big city!

Fifty years after I had lived in a shanty town, I returned there. The *barrio* was now full of nice homes; not upper or even middle-class housing but brick and cement buildings, some highly coloured. Many families had cars. But more recent 'invaders' were living almost at the top of the mountain in primitive huts.

Pope Francis sees hope, not merely as an expectation of future glory but as the attitude of those seeking a better future in this life: migrants who seek a new and better life elsewhere, bringing gifts and talents and labour to their new land. It is their gift to the common good.

Resolution

We live in an impatient world, in a culture of 'must have' and 'have it now'. The poor teach us that we have to await many good things. Pope Francis has proposed a return to a simpler way of life:

> We need to take up an ancient lesson…the conviction that "less is more"… Christian spirituality proposes a growth marked by moderation and the capacity to be happy with little…avoiding the mere accumulation of pleasures.[7]

---

7   Pope Francis, *Laudato sí—Praise Be to You*, (Vatican: LEV, 2015), n 222. (*LS*).

Chapter Six

Humility

So he called a little child to him whom he set among them. Then he said: "Unless you change and become like little children you will never enter the kingdom of heaven."[1]

I was told that in the old days, high in the Andes, when a great landowner (*hacendado*) came up from Lima and visited his hacienda, the peóns[2] would line the track to the great house and bow to him as he was carried aloft on a bier. And a priest, who had worked in the southern highlands, told me that it was not unheard of for a peón to kneel down and kiss the feet of the great landowner.

The hacienda workers were not practising humility; they were humbled because they were oppressed. If you are of little significance, you feel humbled. The poor are the 'little people' because they are insignificant.

When foreign missionaries from prosperous countries went to work among the poor of the Third World's shanty towns and made friends with the poor, the poor felt highly honoured. The ones who were truly honoured were the missionaries! Yet the inferiority complexes of the poor reminded us, as does

---
1   Matt 18:1.
2   A Spanish-American day labourer or unskilled farm worker.

the spirituality of St Térèse de Lisieux, of Jesus' words that demand that his followers imitate the simplicity, dependency and humility of the child.

It is a great joy to live, work and make friends with people who are unpretentious, humble and poor. And if the poor feel honoured that a well-off person from a more prosperous land comes to live among them, the visitor or missionary has nothing to lose and much to gain.

We are God's children and He demands that if we wish to enter His Kingdom (the state of true sonship), we must assume an attitude of childlike simplicity and humility.

I remember being taught in the seminary that humility was the highest of the moral virtues. It is extraordinarily difficult to practise. Self-esteem, personal honour and ambition vie with it. Making "friends with the poor"[3] taught us the value of humility. The humble person is in no way inferior, quite the opposite.

Resolution
Cultivate the virtue of humility in our daily life.

---

[3] Cf. Rom 12:16.

Chapter Seven

Celebration

Peruvians are a festive people. I do not mean the upper or middle classes but the Peruvians of the hills, descendants of Incas and old Spanish 'invaders' and *mestizo*s (of mixed blood). Peasant life is cyclical: the round of crops and harvests, of heat and cold in the high sierras. It is a dull life and the annual sanctoral feast is a relief from it all and a time of high festivity and relaxation from the burden of a harsh land. The annual saint's feast of a village is prepared well in advance by teams of 'majordomos', men and women of the town or village who have the means to finance and organise events. Musicians have to be engaged, the priest booked, fireworks purchased, a bull or even cows readied if there is to be a bullfight.

Drunkenness on the part of the men (women rarely drink alcohol) can almost be excused in view of the drudgery of the rest of the year.

The poor of the mountains brought with them to the city their love of celebration. In the *barriadas*, any excuse was welcomed for a celebration: a house blessing, the blessing of rings for engaged couples, the first cutting of a baby's hair, birthdays, baptisms and weddings. We priests spent many hours a week popping into huts and houses on these occasions, congratulating the family and accepting a soft drink. It was one way of accompanying the poor.

When I visited the straw huts in my Lima shanty town parish, I would be offered a cup of weak tea and a soda biscuit. It was all they could afford. If you are fastidious, it is not always easy to accept what the poor have to offer. The food may not be hygienically cooked, the cook's hands are not always clean and many of their homes have dirt floors. Yet risks must be taken. They felt honoured that a foreign, 'white' priest should deign to cross their threshold; I was the one who felt humbled. I had to cope with what the social scientists call 'culture shock'. But it was a wonderful experience!

Peruvians are an artistic people. They are natural actors and artists and lack the self-consciousness of a more sophisticated people. A three-year-old child will happily stand up and sing or recite in public. Their ancient, colourful dances in rural villages, often telling the story of their exploitation by conquering Spaniards, make beautiful folklore.

In our rather informal parishes on the outskirts of the cities, we are able to adapt the liturgy in many ways—making it lively and meaningful: long processions on Good Friday acting out the Way of the Cross with even a young man being 'crucified', Easter Vigils beginning before dawn leading to baptisms as the sun rises and so on. Vast crowds came and still come to such celebrations, for our people love drama. We heard of one dramatisation of Good Friday through the streets of a Lima *barrio* in which the parish priest acted the part of Jesus. The old Andean peasant women took the flagellation for real and began to stone the 'soldiers'! And they told us of 'virtual reality' celebrations in the mountains in which the actor taking the part of Jesus was truly made to suffer.

Poor parishioners are generous with large amounts of their time in our parishes. Life in the parish is often their principal role in society, and they are proud to act as doormen and collectors, eucharistic ministers and sacristans.

Perhaps because of a greater flexibility in the shanty town parishes it is easy to inculturate the liturgy. It was also easy in the early days of a growing shanty town, where there was no church or hall, to celebrate the Eucharist in the open—on a table placed on the desert floor, with a small congregation standing round and the odd dog under the table.

Poor people quickly learn how to celebrate. They lack the inhibitions of other classes and it is not difficult to recruit catechists, readers, eucharistic ministers and young people for our celebrations. Peasant readers often proclaim the Mass readings far better than more educated people. If our catechists were unable to preach, we provided them with a book of homilies, one of which they could read each Sunday. But they knew their own people and would speak in the local idiom, acknowledging the local way of life.

The Incas honoured the sun god, *Inti*, and celebrated his feast at the summer solstice—June 24 in the southern hemisphere. But the Inca nobles recognised a superior deity, *Wiracocha*. Inca society had three commandments: Don't be lazy, don't steal, don't lie. Theirs was a stable society in which no one went hungry though all the able-bodied had to work. Modern sociologists regard the *Incanato* (Inca Empire) as an excellent example of socialism.

To what extent did the Inca peoples willingly accept Christianity is much debated, but within some sixty years the whole population had been baptised.

The Spanish conquistadors took the Catholicism of sixteenth-century Spain with them and installed it in the Americas. Religious orders attended the faithful in the cities, but the countryside had to make do with occasional visits of a priest and the efforts of simple catechists. The Spanish missionaries also brought with them the popular devotions of Spain—their saints, processions, statues and feast days. Every remote village was given a saint's name and the saint's feast day was to be celebrated with full pomp. This developed into what we call 'popular religion'.

There was a time when this popular religion was much criticised by the clergy, for when religion is mixed with secular festivities it lends itself to drunkenness, superstition and syncretism. Yet this religiosity has sustained the Catholic faith in the Andes throughout the centuries.

When I talk to the young people of the urbanisations, I remind them that here in the city the devotions and traditional feasts of their grandparents are no longer sufficient to sustain the faith where atheists, religious sects, materialism, street violence and political corruption abound. They must develop a more mature faith to contend with the variety of religious options, foreign religious sects, atheism and indifferentism.

Resolution

Our Masses and liturgies should be real celebrations of people's lives, incorporating their customs, problems, hopes and fears.

Chapter Eight

Family and Community

The poor tend to have larger families than other levels of society. Many children are a better guarantee in obtaining income when the children become of working age and of care for the parents when these grow old.

I notice that in the popular housing estates there are always lots of children playing in the streets with a ball or simple toy. This is not so in the more affluent areas of town where the children are indoors playing with their expensive computers and have to be taken to gyms and clubs in their parents' cars.

Whenever we had a party for the children, some would wrap up their slice of cake to take home. They were going to share it with their little brother or sister who had not come to the party. It has been said that the poorest people in the world are the most generous.

When I hiked the hills and mountains of Peru, sometimes a tiny child or a passing peasant would silently hand me an orange or a papaya fruit. And I loved taking Holy Communion to the sick. It meant a walk through the fields to some isolated hut or hamlet and, after attending to the spiritual needs of the sick person, I was always offered a delicious breakfast of fried eggs, bananas and steaming black coffee.

Unfortunately, in the young towns there is much violence against wives and infidelity on the part of husbands in the shanty towns. This is compensated somewhat by friendliness among neighbours and their word for neighbour (*vecino/a*) is common. Then there is an old system of *padrinazgo*.[1] The choice of godparents is highly important. Often the poor will seek out wealthier persons, the employer of the child's father or a local grandee, because this will likely guarantee financial help to the child in the future. The child will hereafter address the godparent as *Padrino* (Godfather) or *Madrina* (Godmother), and a relationship more binding than blood is established.

Friendliness is an important factor in the lives of the poor. In a society where working people have little influence on public affairs, neighbourliness is of great importance. Neighbours receive a warm welcome at the door, and it is also a happy moment when a person meets someone from the same distant province, a *paisano* (fellow countryman/woman). Locals are addressed by their Christian names and a respected older man will be honoured with title of 'Don'.

The poor love the little things: a family gathering, meeting a friend, a walk into the country, a trip to the seaside.

The poor of the shanty towns and remote mountain villages are tolerant of everyone. A disabled villager, perhaps shabbily dressed, might wander into a meeting; no one pushes them out and a place is made for them to sit down. They may not speak but they are a member of the community. They will only be told to be silent if they are drunk or disorderly.

Poor people don't have cars, though they may eventually get hold of a second or third hand vehicle for their work as taxi drivers in the city. Without a car or horse, one uses public transport, or one walks. Peasants walk great distances through the countryside. They walk to market; if they are Catholics, they walk to Sunday Mass; they walk to wakes and meetings. At one of our study weeks in the highlands, a catechist arrived a day late. He had walked for three days from his hamlet to reach us. He spent three days on the course then walked three days back home over the mountains. That meant a loss of more

---

1   From the Spanish, being a godfather (fig.), sponsorship, patronage, protection.

than a week from his fields. I asked him where he had stayed overnight on his long walk. He said people had put him up in their huts and I thought of the hospitality of the rural poor. Sadly, this custom is not so common now in the Peruvian highlands because of terrorism and drug trafficking creating an atmosphere of fear.

It is, of course, easier to welcome the passer-by if you live in a hut in the mountains rather than an elegant flat in the city. In the latter, appointments have to be made before visiting; in the former you can just stroll in. As you approach a homestead in the Peruvian jungle, there is a special 'coo' call as you approach to announce your arrival. You do not enter without being invited. When my neighbours visit me there, they do not knock on the door—it is always open—they just call 'Padre' or 'coo'! In tropical lands, visiting is easy because everyone sits at their door where it is cooler than indoors, and if you are passing by, they are delighted if you just sit and chat for a while. You are very welcome.

In the countryside there is an ancient system of mutual help. When I worked as a priest in the mountains of Peru, we held study days for the rural catechists. They would occasionally come to us beforehand to excuse themselves from attending the next meeting. "I am committed to a *minga*," they would tell us. The *minga* is a traditional system of mutual help. A farmer needs helping hands when he is opening up a field or harvesting. The neighbours help him, and he feeds them that day. When it is the turn of these helpers to work their fields, the man who has been helped has to return the favour. It is a sacred obligation which we had to respect.

Another common word among the poor was 'collaborate'. There is much solidarity among the poor and they feel obliged to collaborate in public works or social activities. When parishes held a garden party or social activity, the people would say: "We must collaborate," that is, we must take part and help in some way.

Resolution

A strict obligation in ancient Israel was to "welcome the stranger."[2]

---

2 Deut 10:19; Lev 19:34.

Value family life and friendship.

Practise loyalty to friends. Be 'neighbour' to those who need us.

Chapter Nine

Communities of Faith

When I began my work as a priest in a Lima shanty town, in spite of the many thousands of people within the parish boundaries, I was anxious to form a Christian community—be it ever so small—a group of families who shared their lives, their problems and their faith. I took as model the report of the apostolic communities as told in the Acts of the Apostles, a text I quoted with great frequency:

> Each day…they met in their houses for the breaking of bread, and they shared their food gladly and generously…Day by day the Lord added to their community those destined to be saved.[1]

My first efforts were an apparent failure.

I invited a small group of women to meet in our straw hut chapel one afternoon after the heat of the sun had diminished. I was there in good time, sitting on some old benches we had acquired. For a long time, there was not a soul in sight. Then one by one, random ladies drifted in. By the time a small group had assembled, it was late afternoon and I knew the women had to be back in their homes to make a meal for their menfolk after their work in the city. I apologised that we had been unable to hold a proper meeting for lack of time. "Not at all,"

---

1   Acts 2:42–47.

they replied, "we have had a lovely time!" We had virtually done nothing, but they had enjoyed themselves, having been invited by their priest and merely coming together and chatting a while. I learned much that afternoon—our values are not their values, little things please and being together is important. That meeting was the beginning of many things: meetings of their menfolk, regular meetings and events for their families, a core Christian community, the start of a new parish, communal work on a hall and parish house; retreats, women's work groups, food kitchens for the poor, and a sense of belonging and being 'Church'.

Core Christian communities sprung up throughout Latin America in the middle of last century. They took different forms and were not always called as such. The poor, whose ancestors had never been listened to in remote mountains or on the great haciendas, were now learning and being heard in Christian study groups throughout Latin America. And their opinions were respected. It was "the cry of the poor". Belonging to a community— of a *barrio*, of a parish or religious group, of a club, is of great importance for poor people who have emigrated from their provinces and who often had little or no say in public affairs. Unable to visit expensive restaurants, afford holidays or trips away from home, their whole lives were bound by the workplace and the *barrio*. The core community, parish or club provided friendship, neighbourliness, mutual help and dignity, and Christian hope.

> When we read the Gospel we find a clear indication: not so much our friends and wealthy neighbours, but above all the poor and the sick, those who are usually despised and overlooked, "those who cannot repay you" (Lk 14:14). There can be no room for doubt or for explanations which weaken so clear a message. Today and always "the poor are the privileged recipients of the Gospel" ... we have to state without mincing words, that there is an inseparable bond between our faith and the poor.[2]

Strong words of Pope Francis!

Working in the shanty towns of the developing world gave us the opportunity to share in the formation of communities of faith. It was not simply a matter of constructing church buildings and parishes but rather of forming cells of committed Christians. We modelled them on the stories of the very first

---

[2] *EG*, n 48.

communities spoken of in the Acts of the Apostles, especially when celebrating Mass in a house, in the open air or in a small chapel with few people present. To celebrate the Eucharist in a poor house, in a hut or in the open air under a tree, with just a few neighbours is a great joy for the celebrant and the people for God who live in a slum, on a refuse dump or shanty town.

The poor need to feel part of a local community, to feel needed. They have often had to fight authorities and police to obtain land and defend their townships; today many have gated areas to prevent gangs of thieves gaining access to their hard-won homes. The homes of the rich are protected by armed guards; the huts of the poor are protected by mongrels and neighbours.

> The joys and the hopes, the griefs and the anxieties of the men of this age, **especially those who are poor** [author's emphasis] or in any way afflicted, these too are the joys and hopes, the griefs and anxieties of the followers of Christ[3]

Resolution

Are our parishes real communities? What does this mean in practice?

Apart from attendance at Sunday Mass, should I belong to some active Christian community?

---

3 GS, n 1.

Chapter Ten

The Wisdom and Ingenuity of the Poor

Wise missionaries do not go to the poor in foreign lands carrying their own wisdom and learning. They go to learn.

A visitor to Peru once told me the story of his watching a man fishing on the shore of a jungle lake. When the fisherman had caught a just a few fish he began to collect his tackle and prepare to leave. The visitor was surprised that the man didn't continue to fish for there was an abundance of them in the lake. "Why don't you continue and sell the fish you don't need?" he asked. "Why should I do that?" answered the man. "You could make money and better your life," was the reply. "And why should I do that?" said the fisherman. "You could become quite rich with the money you make," explained the visitor. "But I am content enough as it is," came the response.

Many years ago, the priests in Lima organised cooperatives for the poor, helping people who didn't understand bank accounts to save. One member of the cooperative was caught stealing funds. At a public meeting the foreign parish priest began to upbraid him. Then someone said: "Just a minute, Padre," and took over. In a long-drawn-out way, he spoke to the culprit without accusations. But the message was clear, face had been saved and the missionary priest had learned much.

The poor know their place. One day our shanty town parishioners went on an outing to a beach resort. On alighting from a dilapidated hired bus, I began to walk to the beach. The parishioners said: "No Padre, we don't go to that beach," and they made for another. The beach I was making for was for the wealthy.

In the settlements, priests would sit through lengthy meetings, often not commenting but accompanying and supporting the people. On one occasion they elected me 'fiscal' at the assembly of the township's committee. I asked what it meant. They told me that I was the one to keep order during the meetings. These took place late on Saturday evenings and would begin quite formally and orderly. But as the evening wore on, things crescendoed. One midnight, things were getting out of hand, so I stood up to restore order. No one took the slightest notice, so I excused myself and went home—I had an early Mass next day!

The 'invaders' of waste lands usually build their own homes. They do this on Sundays, their only free day. The first task is to dig the foundations of their houses, which is relatively easy in the desert. Then, perhaps calling on the assistance of a neighbour or relative who had some experience in building, they put up the brick walls. The laying of a concrete roof required teams of men who mixed the cement and carried old petrol cans full of cement mixture up a ramp to spread on the roof. It all had to be helped with crates of beer.

My parishioners taught me how to obtain land for the parish buildings and then how to construct them. In the mountains they taught me how to find my way through their forests, how to cross rivers and how to solve a thousand problems.

In those days the shanty town dwellers were immensely creative and masters of improvisation: if you hadn't a jack to lift up your car, you just dug a hole under it in the sand; if you hadn't a hammer, you used a stone; if you hadn't a spade, you used your machete. The poor learn to make do with what they have. If they do not have nice new appliances, they make do with old ones. If their worn-out electrical machines don't work, there is always a 'little man' somewhere who can repair them. When the springs of a vehicle broke down in the mountains, they tied them up with branches! When a family in our remote village couldn't afford a coffin to lay a tiny baby, the local handyman put the little infant in his violin case during the wake.

There used to be men in England whom we called 'rag-and-bone men'. They were men who pushed a cart round a housing estate shouting for things the householders wanted to throw away: old washing machines, furniture, clothes, whatever. They could use the cast-offs in some way and make a few pence. These people still exist in the shanty towns. They push their carts around, ring a bell or horn to attract attention and accept anything the neighbours want to throw away.

Similarly, there is a poor living to be made on rubbish dumps on the outskirts of the cities, where people, sometimes with children, put up with the smell or rotting refuse to glean whatever will bring in a few coppers.

Poor children are highly inventive in using cast-offs to play with: adapting old boxes, wheels or garden tools to entertain themselves. They play in the streets if there is not too much traffic, while the children of the better-off classes remain indoors with their computers or wait to be taken to exclusive clubs and swimming pools.

In the urban settlements the word they used for 'plumber' was 'gasfitter', and every able male was regarded as something of a gasfitter! Though occasionally there were tragedies when a young fellow, attempting to steal electricity, would climb up to a power cable and electrocute himself.

Eventually, after years of planning, struggling and cajoling of public authorities, the 'invasions' were supplied with amenities, and hopefully the missionaries had helped in some way by their presence and support.

A woman in my shanty town parish, looking back after years in the *barrio*, said: "We started with nothing and struggled, and now we have our homes and our community, and we did it all ourselves."

Resolution

Only buy what is really needed.

Use goods until they have lost their use or value.

How can we live a life of simplicity in the modern world?

Chapter Eleven

Environment

The Spaniards and Portuguese took over the lands of native peoples in South America, the northern Europeans the lands of Africa and North America. The poor owned the land in many continents until the rich and powerful came.

The rich consume more than the poor. They consume more goods and land, though the poor are mainly responsible for the land and it is they, the poor, who suffer the effects of environmental degradation more than others. The rich and powerful deprive the poor of natural resources—land, water, timber—and once having extracted what they need, leave the environment barren and useless. Pope Francis writes:

> The impact of present [ecological] imbalances is also seen in the premature death of many of the poor, in conflict sparked by the shortage or resources and in any number of other problems which are insufficiently represented on global agendas.[1]

I myself have seen the loss of prime forests in the Amazon basin, the sad barrenness of despoiled land and the rivers running with oil and sludge. Rural people know their environment and do it less damage than others, less than industrialists, gold prospectors, largescale farmers, transport owners.

---

1   *LS*, n 48.

When I lived on the edge of a jungle city with a garden which not long since had been rainforest, there were still many plants there, and whenever I felt unwell or my dogs had a sore, there was always a natural remedy to hand which my neighbours could identify. No one knows how many plants there are in the rainforest, several possibly offering remedies for our illnesses. My neighbours knew many of them. The natural riches of the rainforests could be lost forever if the environmental depredation continues. One of my hobbies in the jungle was to catalogue the birds of which there are some 1,700 species in Peru. I identified sixty different species in my garden alone.

Peasants are intimate with the land, its fields, trees, animals and produce. When we held study days for our rural catechists, we would sometimes talk about the environment. I used to introduce the topic, but the peasant catechists would take over and then direct the whole debate. They knew far more than I did.

The poor recycle the cast-offs from the wealthy. The rich buy what they don't need, the poor only purchase necessities. They make use of what others regard as throwaways. They will gratefully accept any artefact, piece of furniture or clothing which the wealthier want to get rid of. The poor have fewer clothes and wear them longer, they make use of the cast-offs of the wealthy and their animals consume food residue. They purchase the old cars of wealthier drivers and use them as taxis to earn a living. And though they cannot buy beautiful things—woollen garments, gold and silver trinkets, paintings and leather goods—they make them to sell to the rich and the tourists!

The poor eat to sustain life; the rich eat the delicacies their bodies don't need. The poor eat to survive; the rich eat for pleasure.

Resolution

Small is beautiful and today we have to learn to live more sustainably and reduce the breach between rich and poor. Pope Francis has proposed a return to a simpler lifestyle:

> We need to take up an ancient lesson…the conviction that "less is more"… Christian spirituality proposes a growth marked by moderation and the capacity to be happy in little…avoiding the accumulation of pleasures.[2]

---

2   LS, n 222.

Am I sufficiently concerned about the destruction of natural earth resources, the oceans, the rain forests, the icecaps?

Is there anything I can do to avoid contaminating the earth with plastic waste, with non-biodegradable materials?

Could I create a small eco-friendly plot or garden?

Chapter Twelve

Silence

Be still and acknowledge that I am God.[1]
"We need to practise the art of listening which is more than simply hearing." [2]

I wish I could say that the poor had taught me the value of silence. Yet they have in a way: through their noise!

For, once in the city, and as soon as their purses allow, the people from the silent mountains buy the largest music system with the most powerful loudspeakers which are switched on, if not all day, with great frequency. When they have a fiesta, they hire even larger speakers so that the whole neighbourhood is bombarded with popular music throughout the night.

Where has the silence gone? Modern life is so noisy we cannot hear anything! Pop music in supermarkets, the pulsing thrum of a car radio, the volume of a neighbour's television, the roar of an aeroplane, police sirens, the blare of loudspeakers...My friends used to invite me to parties where it was impossible to converse because of pop music from loudspeakers which hurt the ears.

---

1   Ps 46:10.
2   *EG*, n 171.

And in the shanty towns, there is always some neighbour celebrating, building or hammering.

And noise need not be only audial: multitasking, overloaded with commitments, news, can be just as distracting.

Thus, in an excessively noisy, overstimulated world, the Christian must seek peace and silence. God may be found for some in agitation and activity, but for most He will be better found where Elijah found Him: in the "small breeze" (1Kgs 19:12).

Rudolf Otto quotes W. James as an example of this: "The perfect stillness of the night was thrilled by a more solemn silence… I could not any more have doubted that *He* was there than that I was."[3]

It is commonplace to talk about our noisy world, but we should not identify noise only with decibels. There are many kinds of 'sounds': agitation, travel, headlines, a hectic lifestyle, conversations, parties, business meetings, concerts, dances, television, radio, headphones, electronic gadgets…

In a beautiful address at Nazareth, Pope Paul VI spoke of silence:

> We learn [from Nazareth] its silence. If only we could appreciate again its great value. We need this wonderful state of mind, beset as we are, by the cacophony of strident protests and conflicting claims so characteristic of these turbulent times. The silence of Nazareth should teach us how to meditate in peace and quiet, to reflect on the deeply spiritual, and to be open to the voice of God's inner wisdom and the counsel of his true teachers.[4]

High in the beautiful grasslands of the White Mountains (*Cordillera Blanca*) of northern Peru, I met an elderly peasant woman, all alone, dressed in the colourful blouse and skirts of the highland women, watching her sheep in

---

3 R. Otto, *The Idea of the Holy*, translated by John W. Harvey, (London: Oxford University Press, 1958, repr. 1979), 22-23, citing William James, *The Varieties of Religious Experience: A Study on Human Nature*, Being the Gifford Lectures on Natural Religion, delivered at Edinburgh in 1901-1902, p.66.
4 Pope Paul VI, *Visit to the Basilica of the Annunciation in Nazareth*, January 5, 1964.

total silence—a lovely example of the 'good shepherd'. I wondered whether she would prefer the noise of the town in the valley below!

I don't think my Peruvian friends appreciate silence. They are great talkers. Nor can they cope with solitude: they cannot live alone; peasants sleep all huddled together in their huts sometimes among the animals against the cold mountain air.

Jesus loved solitude and silence: he escaped at dawn into the hills in search of it.[5] He prayed to the Father in the silence of the night. The great saints, especially those who went into the deserts, searched out solitude and silence. Monks get up in the silence of the night to pray their communal Matins; contemplatives pray at night, and it is not surprising that, in our strident world, the number of hermits is increasing today. And astronauts have surely discovered the silence of space.

Infant teachers get their pupils to 'listen' to the silence. Babies need silence though few seem to get it nowadays. And I remember being told that one of my grandfathers used to say: silence is golden.

> *Elected Silence, sing to me*
> *And beat upon my whorlèd ear,*
> *Pipe me to pastures still and be*
> *The music that I care to hear.*[6]

I love the tale of the Desert Father who received a bishop in his hermitage but uttered to him not a word. When the visitor had departed the young monk attending the old Abba asked him why he hadn't spoken to the visitor who had made a special visit to hear his wisdom. The old man replied: "If he wasn't impressed by my silence, he wouldn't have been impressed by my words!"

Yet for some, escape into silence may be impossible. In which case, the one who prays has to learn the art of prayer among the noise, like the Benedictine monk who spent years in a cell in Vietnam among criminals but who was able

---

5   Mk 1:35.
6   G.M. Hopkins, 'The Habit of Perfection' in Id. *Poems of Gerard Manley Hopkins*, (London: Humphrey Milford, 1928).

to engage in deep prayer by using the noise, the shouting and the discomforts as fuel for his prayer. He turned everything into prayer.

Only the silent hear.

Resolution

Learn from the heron who stands silently still in the water awaiting his meal.

Switch off radio and television if we are not really listening or watching; don't always be talking, communicating, texting.

Jesus calmed the storm; we must calm the storms in our lives.

We enter our room (cell) and, as one of the Desert Fathers, Abba Moses, said, "Go, sit in your cell, and your cell will teach you everything."[7]

---

7   Cf. *The Sayings of the Desert Fathers*, translated by Sr Benedicta Ward SLG, (Michigan: Cistercian Publication, 1975).

Chapter Thirteen

Accompanying the Poor

Pope Francis has talked about the "art of accompaniment".[1] He also commented:

> Our commitment does not consist exclusively in activities or programmes of promotion and assistance…but [in an] attentiveness…a true concern for their person…to seek their good. This entails appreciating the poor in the goodness, in their experience of life, in their culture and their ways of living the faith.[2]

A great amount of our time in the shanty towns was taken up accompanying the poor. Although missionaries can try to alleviate the poor in their extreme needs, Pope Francis points out that the missionary task is not so much to help the poor to rise out of their poverty and join the middle classes, but rather to help them understand that God has a special place for them 'in his heart'. So, we listen to them and accept their friendship. Friendliness and attention are forms of charity.

When Irish, Anglo-Saxon and North American missionaries went to Latin America in the middle of last century, they soon realised that it was the people of the shanty towns themselves who had to solve most of their own problems. And though their origins were as simple peasants from mountain

---

1   *EG*, n 169.
2   ibid., n 199.

provinces, they were very competent in tackling their affairs. They turned out to be extremely capable organisers; they knew what they wanted, and they were determined to get it. But the missionaries could accompany them in their struggles.

One way in which we did this was to join their committees, sit, listen and sometimes suggest. When they formed a commission to go into the big city in search of government ministers, company directors and military officers to request public services, we went with them. Very often the man behind the large desk had been educated in an expensive school run by religious and would spend time chatting with the priest or sister about their religious education, but eventually, as is the way in Latin America after laboured introductions, we would come to the point and explain the reason for the visit. The presence of an educated, religious foreigner lent weight to the visit and the request.

Hence a large part of the priest's work in the settlements included accompanying the people in their joys and sorrows. He was very much part of the lives of the *barrio* and lived close to them in the centre of the community or 'invasion'. The parish office would be busy with parishioners the whole day arranging sacraments, seeking material help, requesting a note to an assistance agency. It was a way of getting to know the parishioners and their problems.

> From the dust he lifts up the lowly,
>
> From the dung heap he raises the poor.[3]

Resolution

Visit the elderly and the poor of your district. Is there anything you could do to alleviate their poverty, loneliness?

---

3   Ps 113:7.

Chapter Fourteen

Hospitality

A strict obligation in ancient Israel was to "welcome the stranger."[1]

Although poor people like to give gifts to their visitor, the best gift is their friendship, attention and interest in you. This only costs them time, and they have plenty of that. They are never too busy to meet and greet the stranger or visitor. There is no 'inconvenient' time to visit them, and they would never tell you that your visit is untimely.

Peruvians love fiestas, but if you visit the poor at another time, all they may be able to offer is a cup of tea and a soda biscuit, and that is what I used to be offered on my rounds in the shanty town. They share what little they have. Although when I visited villages in the highlands where there was rural produce, I was fed enormous quantities of food.

There is a very poor family I know in the city where I lived in the Amazon. Their twenty-three-year-old son is totally incapacitated and only recognises his parents. They care for him with love and affection and struggle to cover the cost of his medication. They always invite me to a meal when I visit the city. The meal is a simple one of fish and bananas, and I listen to their story of life's struggle. As I leave, they load me with fruit. The parents have stuck together

---

1   Deut 10:19; Lev 19:34.

through the years, in spite of homelessness, poverty and sickness when so many other men would have abandoned the mother of their children. I have enormous respect for that family.

Resolution

To visit the sick and housebound; it is the best gift we can give them.

Chapter Fifteen

Suffering

"He has lifted up the lowly," sang Mary in her Magnificat.

One day in our coastal shanty town a mother ran out of her hut to make a brief purchase at a nearby stall. She left her baby and the paraffin stove burning in her straw hut. The hut caught fire and it took all the delicate force of our religious sisters to prevent the mother from seeing the charcoal remains of her little one.

I think the poor understand suffering better than others. They realise that it is part of the package of life and of their Christian faith.

There is just one major cancer hospital in the whole of Peru. It is in the capital city, Lima. It is always crowded with hundreds of poor people, many from remote provinces in the mountains: they await their turn to see doctors, queue for medicines, sit outside the buildings or doss down on the grass verges where many of their relatives, who have nowhere to stay, sleep overnight. One sees horrendous sores and growths. Some of the patients and relatives from far away provinces might be fortunate enough to get accommodation in the few hostels available for them. I wondered where the better-off people went for their treatment, for everyone I see in this huge emporium of suffering are the 'little people'.

Following the devastating Peruvian earthquake of 1970, I was a member of a rescue team that travelled high above the coastal clouds into the mountains. The injured were mainly children whose open wounds had been caused by falling beams in their adobe houses.[1] We treated them as best we could before they were evacuated to better medical help in Lima. Following the earthquake, the authorities told the mountain people to put more straw into their adobe bricks. The poor had suffered like the ancient Hebrews in Pharaoh's Egypt.

The poor understand Good Friday better than Easter Sunday. Our Good Friday liturgies are packed, the Easter Vigil not as much. The lugubrious, black-stoled statues of the Sorrowful Mother in Good Friday processions are followed by huge crowds of the faithful in Latin America. The lot of Mary at the foot of the cross is so often their lot too. Jesus' concern for the sick occupies almost as much space in the Gospels as his teaching: the blind see, the disabled walk.[2]

It saddens me when I am called to attend a sick, elderly person who has come from some remote village and now lives with sons or daughters in a strange urban land. They sometimes only speak the old Inca tongue, *Quechua*, and we cannot communicate with them. They are strangers in their own land.

It is a truism to say that suffering is a part of human life; it is certainly part of a Christian life. Occasionally one meets people who have enjoyed robust health all their lives: they have had the good fortune never to suffer more than the occasional cold nor have had to contend with life's problems. There was something lacking in their lives. A Christian who never suffers either physically or psychologically, will find it hard to understand the cross. The crucifix adorns our walls but has to be lived. All the saints suffered—even those who lived in comfortable convents and apparently had 'no worries in the world'! St Paul has a curious passage in his letter to the Colossians: he talks about "making up the sufferings of Christ".[3] He cannot mean that Christ's sufferings were inadequate, but that we have a part to share in them.

---

[1] A building material made from earth and organic materials. *Adobe* is Spanish for mudbrick.
[2] Cf. Matt 11:5; Lk 7:22; Isa 35:5.
[3] Col 1:24.

Resolution

For the Christian, suffering is part of the Christian 'package'; sharing the cross. There is no escape from it. It can be physical, mental, loneliness, sadness, concern…and must be added to our Christian life.

Chapter Sixteen

Death

In one of his talks to us in Lima, Fr Gutiérrez commented that the poor die before their due time. They die because they often live far from hospitals and because they lack the resources for medication and surgical treatment.

When I was a parish priest in a Lima shanty town, I would receive parishioners in a little office in my house. I always asked them where they came from; they were nearly all from mountain provinces and I could sometimes guess their standard of education or poverty. The people from the most underdeveloped highland districts were often unable to sign their names. Some would say to me that they were now old. When I asked how old, they replied that they were in their forties! I was often older than my visitors and still felt young! They knew they were ageing.

Deaths were frequent in the *barriadas*—of old people who had come down from the mountains with sons and daughters, infant mortality, accidents, deaths from violence and police brutality. Baptisms of dying babies were almost a daily task, and we were always asked to pray at the wake in the home of the deceased where relatives, neighbours and friends sat around the coffin all night and until the burial next day. On those occasions all we could do was quietly shake hands with everyone, say a few prayers, perhaps say a few words about the meaning of death for Christians and express our condolences to the family.

One day, in one of the poorest and roughest parts of our city parish, a boy of twelve was playing ball and got thirsty. There was a dirty stream running nearby and he took a drink from it. Next day he was dead. The family were so poor they couldn't afford a proper funeral or burial plot, so I accompanied them as they carried the body up into the desert hills and (perhaps illegally) buried the body there among the silence of the hills.

Poor people prefer to die at home in the village where they have been brought up. If they are being treated in a distant hospital, they ask to be taken back home when they realise death is near. Back in their adobe huts they lie on a bed or on the mud floor supported by a daughter or sister if they need help in breathing or coughing or their perspiration needs wiping away. The relatives and neighbours they have known all their lives crowd into the house or hut, children and the curious lounge in the doorway.

Peruvian law stipulates that the funeral must take place within twenty-four hours because of the tropical heat. In the countryside the whole village attends it. There is often wailing (*keening*) at the graveside which stops for prayers to be said. In some villages the deceased's house will be open for nine days following the burial, during which the deceased's clothes are laid out, prayers said by a catechist and all visitors fed—customs that go back centuries perhaps with the belief that the soul needs that space of time to leave this world. If a priest is available sometime later, relatives of the deceased will ask for a Mass to be offered for their dead.

One day I went to anoint an elderly man in his hut in the fields and was surprised to see a coffin leaning against the wall near his bed. He knew what was coming and was quite resigned. He wouldn't have known that he was imitating the Russian hermit, St Seraphim of Sarov, who also kept a coffin in his hut, or the many saints who kept a skull near them.

On the eve of All Souls Day, November 2, relatives visit the graves of their dead. They take flowers and, in some places, food which is left on the grave— an old belief perhaps from pagan times. I always accompanied the crowds on that afternoon to offer prayers. It was impossible to pray at each individual grave, as the people would have liked, so I prayed for all those buried there, *urbi et orbi*. This didn't satisfy everyone, so there was usually an old fellow with a squeaky violin who supplied a dirge at individual graves and charged a fee.

If the poor do die "before their due time", I think the meaning of death is better understood by them than by many others.

Resolution
Learn to face the fact of our own death with equanimity and hope.

Chapter Seventeen

Gracias

The well-known spiritual writer Henri Nouwen spent a few months in a Peruvian shanty town. When he returned home, he wrote of his experiences in a book entitled 'Gracias',[1] because he said that in the *barriadas* of Lima he had learned to say '*gracias*', thanks. That little word is constantly on the lips of the people of the shanties. I must have heard it thousands of times on the lips of the poor.

We should praise God for everything, even for things that are apparently not so good.[2] We often don't know which things are bad and which are good. Our English proverb "It's an ill wind that blows no good" is similar in Spanish: "There is no evil that doesn't bring some good". So, we should praise God for all things.

I once visited an elderly aunt-in-law who was coming to the end of her life. She was blind and extremely deaf and had to be attended daily by four carers. Her son shouted to her that I was visiting and all she replied was: "God is good, God is good." I realised I was in the presence of great sanctity.

---

1 H.J.M. Nouwen, *Gracias!: A Latin American Journal*, (New York: Harper & Row, 1983).
2 The Charismatic Renewal taught us this.

In his book on St Francis, Chesterton commented that Francis "understood down to its very depths the theory of thanks, and its depths are a bottomless abyss."[3]

Living among the poor we learned much from those struggling in poverty, sickness and tragedy: hopefully we helped them in their struggle. However, though the poor may not have realised it, those of us who worked with them were radically changed, not merely by having to live more simply and renounce many things, but in understanding the scriptures, theology and celebration in a new way. We went to them because we thought they needed us; we needed them more than they needed us! And we were deeply grateful for the experience.

Resolution

Thank God for everything: even for what is apparently not so good.

---

3   G.K. Chesterton, *Saint Francis of Assisi*, (London: Hodder & Stoughton, nd), 182.

Chapter Eighteen

World Day of the Poor

In 2017, Pope Francis created the World Day of the Poor to be celebrated on the thirty-third Sunday of Ordinary time.[1]

In a large parish on the outskirts of the city of Lima, site of one of the largest urban sprawls of South America, and once site of a celebrated invasion of barren land by the poor, the parish priest invited all the elderly, sick and poor—many of whom have followed their sons and daughters from their mountain villages and who feel alienated now in the great city—to a day of celebration. The early morning Mass, said in the open air in a spirit of joy, was followed by breakfast. Then doctors, dentists, nurses, masseurs and barbers provided attention while a band played the haunting music of the Andes for those who wanted to dance. Lunch was served for everyone, and in the afternoon the people gradually wandered slowly back to their half-built homes.

On the wall of the great church, where these poor people had enjoyed their day, are written in large letters the words:

> *Come to me, all you who labour and are over-burdened,*
> *and I will give you rest.*[2]

---

[1] In his message to the second World Day of the Poor, Pope Francis commented that the poor are the first people capable of recognising the presence of God and can testify to God's presence in their lives.

[2] Matt 11:28.